CINDERELLA III
41360

Which are you:
a Princess, a Villain, or an Animal?

Find out with these great books
from DK Publishing!

www.kiddk.com

Princess

THE ESSENTIAL GUIDE

Contents

Introduction

BY ROYAL DECREE YOU ARE INVITED TO MEET all your favorite Disney Princesses in this beautiful Essential Guide. Learn about sweet and gentle Snow White, adventurous Ariel, feisty Jasmine, charming Belle, kind-natured Aurora, and caring Cinderella. Read all about the things they love to do, their closest friends and their many adventures.

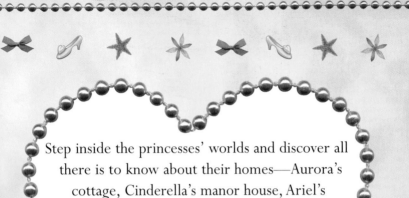

Step inside the princesses' worlds and discover all there is to know about their homes—Aurora's cottage, Cinderella's manor house, Ariel's underwater castle, and Jasmine's palace. Also follow the journeys of Snow White and Belle through their enchanting lands. Enjoy this special guide to the Disney Princesses and their magical worlds— where dreams come true!

Snow White

WITH HAIR AS BLACK as
ebony, lips as red
as roses, and skin as white as snow,
this lovely princess is perfectly named
Snow White. Not only is she beautiful
but she is sweet-natured, too. Everyone
loves her except, of course, her vain and
jealous stepmother, the Queen.

Her favorite things

Singing and dancing always cheer
Snow White up, and give her
courage when she's afraid.

Telling stories is one of Snow
White's great talents. The Seven
Dwarfs like to listen to her stories
about the day her prince will
come and how they will live
happily in a beautiful castle.

The animals and
birds of the forest
love Snow White's kind
and gentle nature.
They even help her clean
up the Dwarfs' messy cottage!

Her hair is as black as ebony.

Her lips are as red as roses.

The lining of her sleeves match her hair ribbon.

ABOUT SNOW WHITE

♥ She's so sweet and gentle, she makes lots of friends wherever she goes.

♥ She is always cheerful and looks on the bright side.

♥ She is romantic and longs to meet her true love.

♥ She is practical and works hard.

Snow White loves to walk in the Enchanted Forest and pick the pretty flowers. But she can't bring too many into the cottage because flowers make Sneezy sneeze!

When the Dwarfs find out that Snow White is a good cook, they are delighted. Even more so when they discover she can bake their favorite gooseberry pie!

Snow White sews her own petticoats to wear underneath her dresses.

Oh, it's adorable!

🎀 *Love and romance*

It seems like Snow White's wish for love will never come true, spending all her time working hard for the Queen.

But love always finds a way and even in her tattered rags, the Prince is captivated by Snow White's beauty.

Snow White's world

SNOW WHITE LIVES IN AN ENCHANTED land with seven jeweled hills and seven waterfalls. Beyond the farthest hill stands the castle where she grew up with her wicked stepmother, the Queen. From here you can see the pretty little cottage where the Seven Dwarfs live.

In disguise, the Queen sets off by boat to find Snow White.

The Queen's laboratory and dungeons lie below the castle.

✿ Running away

In the Dark Forest, even the trees seem to be against Snow White as she runs away from the Queen.

Snow White has nowhere to go and gets lost in the dense forest. Eventually she can run no farther and she falls to the ground in tears.

The clearing where Snow White meets the friendly forest animals

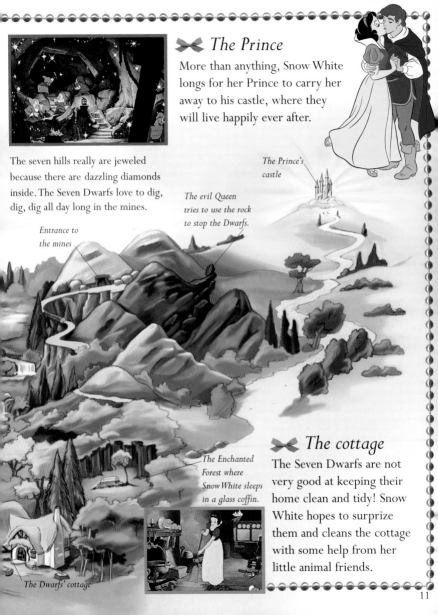

The Prince

More than anything, Snow White longs for her Prince to carry her away to his castle, where they will live happily ever after.

The seven hills really are jeweled because there are dazzling diamonds inside. The Seven Dwarfs love to dig, dig, dig all day long in the mines.

The Prince's castle

The evil Queen tries to use the rock to stop the Dwarfs.

Entrance to the mines

The Enchanted Forest where Snow White sleeps in a glass coffin.

The cottage

The Seven Dwarfs are not very good at keeping their home clean and tidy! Snow White hopes to surprize them and cleans the cottage with some help from her little animal friends.

The Dwarfs' cottage

Friends and enemies

ONE OF THE GREAT GIFTS Snow White has is the ability to make friends easily; the animals and Dwarfs would do anything for her. Even Grumpy! But the Queen is madly jealous of her naturally beautiful stepdaughter. And the cruel Queen is a very dangerous enemy to have.

Her enemies

As well as being Snow White's stepmother, the Queen is also a wicked witch. She hates Snow White so much that she uses a poisoned apple to try and get rid of her.

'Magic Mirror on the wall, who is the fairest one of all?'

The Magic Mirror must answer all the questions that the jealous Queen asks.

Despite being pure evil, the Queen has a cold beauty.

The poisoned apple

Before turning red, for a moment the apple reveals the poison that covers it.

Although the Huntsman is a loyal servant of the Queen, he is not really wicked. Seeing Snow White's sweet nature, he cannot bear to carry out the Queen's order to kill the innocent princess.

❈ Her friends

The Seven Dwarfs and the birds and animals that meet Snow White love

her dearly. They try to protect her from the wicked Queen and her evil spells.

Grumpy Doc Bashful Sneezy Happy Dopey Sleepy

A wish comes true

From the moment that Snow White becomes more beautiful than the Queen, her life is in danger. Although the Seven Dwarfs try their best, they cannot protect her from the Queen's black magic. But good is stronger than evil, and in the end the Prince's love for Snow White saves the day.

One spring morning

Snow White sings while she cleans. The Prince hears her and falls in love.

I beg of you, your Highness, forgive me!

The Magic Mirror tells the Queen that Snow White is the fairest in the land. The Queen orders the Huntsman to take the princess out to pick flowers in the forest and kill her.

Although he tries, the Huntsman can't bring himself to harm her and tells Snow White to run away. She flees and hides in the little cottage in the forest.

The cottage is owned by the Seven Dwarfs. When they come home to find a stranger in their home, they are afraid. But as soon as they meet Snow White, they want her to stay with them forever.

✄ The poisoned apple

Disguised as an ugly old peddler woman, the Queen persuades trusting Snow White to take one bite of the poisoned apple. She promises this will make all her dreams come true.

No harm can come to Snow White now that her Prince has come.

There's nobody like him anywhere at all.

As soon as Snow White takes a bite of the apple, she falls to the ground in a deep sleep and cannot be woken. When the Dwarfs find her they place her in a special glass coffin, and keep a vigil at her side.

The Prince finds Snow White in the forest and wakes her from her slumber with true love's kiss. They set off for his palace and a future filled with happiness.

Cinderella

FROM THE MOMENT HER BELOVED FATHER dies, poor Cinderella is made to work as a servant by her cruel Stepmother and spoiled stepsisters. But she never stops hoping and believing that one day her life will change and a handsome young prince will sweep her off her feet.

Her friends

Although they are only tiny mice, Gus and Jaq are Cinderella's loyal friends. They help with her chores and save her from being lonely.

ABOUT CINDERELLA

♥ She is cheerful and sunny, no matter how difficult things are.

♥ Cinderella is hard-working and practical and can cook and sew.

♥ She is very caring, and her heart is full of kindness.

Delicate lace petticoat

The Fairy Godmother makes Cinderella's dreams of happiness come true. Her magic spell makes it possible for Cinderella to go to the ball, even if it is only for a few hours.

The long, flowing skirt, made of shimmering sky-blue satin, reflects the color of her eyes.

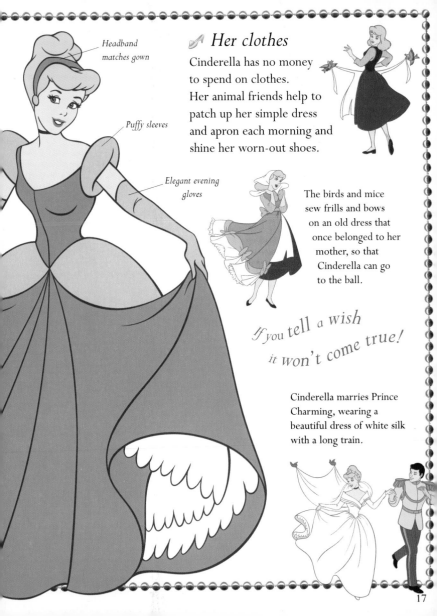

Headband matches gown

Puffy sleeves

Elegant evening gloves

✎ *Her clothes*

Cinderella has no money
to spend on clothes.
Her animal friends help to
patch up her simple dress
and apron each morning and
shine her worn-out shoes.

The birds and mice
sew frills and bows
on an old dress that
once belonged to her
mother, so that
Cinderella can go
to the ball.

*If you tell a wish
it won't come true!*

Cinderella marries Prince
Charming, wearing a
beautiful dress of white silk
with a long train.

17

Home sweet home

Cinderella's tiny attic bedroom

ONCE UPON A TIME, the manor house was the happiest place in the whole of the kingdom. But when Cinderella's mean Stepmother arrives, things change. Lady Tremaine makes Cinderella sleep in the attic and do household chores all day long.

While her father is alive, the house is happy.

Home life

Cinderella can see the beautiful castle from her bedroom window, and she imagines how wonderful it would be to live there.

Door to courtyard

The kitchen where Cinderella spends much of her day cooking and cleaning

Mouse hole

Every morning Cinderella feeds the animals before she takes breakfast up to her Stepmother, in bed.

Family and friends

Jaq and Gus care deeply for Cinderella. The same cannot be said for her family; she waits on them hand and foot without any thanks!

Lady Tremaine and her spoiled daughters, Drizella and Anastasia, hate Cinderella because of her natural beauty.

Doors to Drizella and Anastasia's grand bedrooms

Lady Tremaine's bedroom is three times bigger than Cinderella's attic room.

Lucifer's velvet bed

Lucifer the cat lies in wait for the mice to torment them. Even Cinderella, who loves most animals, hasn't a good word to say about him!

Music room

Magic moments

A LITTLE MAGIC IS ALL Cinderella needs to find happiness after her father dies. She has charm and beauty, and all the elegance of a princess, and with a little help from her Fairy Godmother her dreams come true.

The invitation

To celebrate the Prince's return, all eligible ladies in the land are invited to attend a ball at the castle.

Cinderella's ugly stepsisters cannot bear to see her looking so beautiful in her mother's dress. They are so jealous they tear her outfit to pieces.

With a wave of her magic wand, the Fairy Godmother ensures that Cinderella can go to the ball.

🥿 The ball

As soon as their eyes meet at the ball, Cinderella and the Prince fall in love. But when the clock strikes twelve, Cinderella leaves her glass slipper behind

on the stairs in her hurry to leave before the magic ends. Soon her dress turns into rags.

Cinderella's golden hair is swept up on her head and she looks like a real princess.

The Grand Duke is absolutely delighted when Cinderella produces the matching glass slipper and slips it on to her dainty foot. Lady Tremaine, on the other hand, is furious.

Magic is in the air!

🥿 The wedding

After all his searching, Prince Charming has at last found the beautiful girl he danced with at the ball. The whole kingdom rejoices when he marries Cinderella.

Aurora

BROUGHT UP IN THE COUNTRYSIDE, this sweet and gentle girl has no idea that she is really a princess named Aurora. She learns the truth on her sixteenth birthday, the same day that, due to a curse put on her by a wicked fairy, she falls into an enchanted sleep. Only true love's first kiss saves her from eternal slumber.

ABOUT AURORA

♥ She's gentle and sweet-natured. All who know her love her.

♥ Aurora is thoughtful and unspoiled. She is always willing to help.

♥ She is a romantic and believes that her dreams of love will one day come true.

Her favorite things

As a baby, Aurora was given the gift of song. Her voice is sweet and pure, and she loves to sing to the animals in the forest.

It takes lots of magic to create this beautiful dress, fit for a very special princess.

Aurora lives in a cottage situated in the heart of a beautiful forest. The woods are her playground where she can think and dream, dip her toes in the stream, and pick sweet berries.

Her hair is the color of golden sunshine.

She is always ready with a smile.

🌹 Her clothes

Growing up in the forest, Aurora has a simple wardrobe, but she is so unspoiled that she doesn't mind. And she is so beautiful that she looks lovely even in the plainest of dresses with just a shawl to wrap around her shoulders.

Her beauty is as natural as a rose in bloom.

If you dream a thing more than once, it's sure to come true!

 The good fairies use their magic to make Aurora a stunning birthday dress. But should it be pink or blue? They just can't decide on the color!

🌹 Her princess dress

When Aurora wears the magical dress and her golden crown, she is transformed from a sheltered young girl into an elegant princess. Now she is ready to marry Prince Phillip and become a beautiful bride.

Forest life

THE GOOD FAIRIES TAKE BABY AURORA to live in a pretty little cottage, deep in the forest, to hide her from the wicked fairy's curse. They rename her Briar Rose after the wild flower that grows in the forest, and they live here happily for sixteen years.

Birthday celebrations

Unlike most princesses, who have servants, Briar Rose begins her birthday by helping her aunts to dust and spring-clean their little cottage!

Flora, Fauna, and Merryweather love Briar Rose dearly and have special plans for her birthday. They ask her to pick berries in the forest so that they can make her a surprize gift.

Briar Rose meets the man of her dreams in the forest and her birthday is the happiest ever. She doesn't realize that the handsome young man is actually a prince.

The bed curtains come from the palace.

The little birds love to visit Briar Rose in her bedroom.

The sound of trickling water lulls Briar Rose to sleep at night.

Sparks of blue and
pink magic escape
from the chimney.

The roof is
made of straw.

Fauna

Flora

Merryweather

Castle life

The chamber where Aurora sleeps peacefully

Her bed is draped in rich velvet.

The spiral staircase leads to the secret chamber.

N AMED AURORA AFTER THE DAWN because she brought sunshine into her proud parents' lives, the baby princess seemed to have all she could wish for. But not for long! At the party given to celebrate her birth, the wicked fairy, Maleficent, promised that Aurora would prick her finger on a spindle and die before the sun set on her sixteenth birthday.

● Baby celebrations

Flora and Fauna bless Aurora with gifts of song and beauty. But Merryweather still has her gift to give when Maleficent arrives.

At the party, King Hubert and King Stefan celebrate the betrothal of their children, Phillip and Aurora.

The good fairies rush to try and save Aurora.

The fire dies down to reveal a secret door to the tower.

Prince Phillip is the only one who can wake Aurora.

Maleficent is very offended when she is not invited to the royal party. She is so angry that she curses the baby Aurora. But Luckily Merryweather has one gift to give and lessens the curse.

Sixteen years later

Maleficent's curse comes true when Aurora pricks her finger on a spinning wheel and falls into a deep sleep. When Prince Phillip tries to save Aurora, Maleficent turns into a fierce dragon—but with the Sword of Truth and Shield of Virtue he defeats her.

Sleeping Beauty

As far as Aurora is concerned, her life has been uneventful. For sixteen years she has lived in the forest longing for excitement and romance, with no friends other than the woodland animals. Then, on her sixteenth birthday, everything seems to happen at once!

The early years

Aurora's life changes forever when Maleficent arrives at the royal party and casts her evil spell.

Briar Rose meets Phillip whilst picking berries in the forest. The handsome young prince is the man of her dreams and they fall head-over-heels in love with each other.

Briar Rose is upset when the fairies tell her that she is a princess. She doesn't want to marry a prince she has never met! She doesn't realize that the prince she is to marry is the man she loves.

Her birthday

As soon as Aurora pricks her finger on the spindle, she feels dizzy and sinks into a deep sleep.

We've met before.

Once upon a dream!

When the fairies find Aurora asleep, they know that the King and Queen will be heartbroken.

Prince Phillip can't take his eyes off the beautiful princess.

The precious golden crown is a present from the good fairies.

The floaty skirt makes her feel like she's dancing on air.

When Phillip kisses Aurora, Maleficent's curse is broken and she wakes from her sleep.

Ariel

PRINCESS ARIEL IS A BEAUTIFUL MERMAID, **and the youngest daughter of Triton, the Sea King.** Ariel's greatest wish is to live like a human on dry land, and she becomes even more determined to realize her dream

the moment she sets eyes upon Prince Eric. Young and headstrong, Ariel usually gets her own way, but there is a price to pay.

Her favorite things

Ariel's best friend is a little fish named Flounder. They go

on many exciting adventures together and often end up in lots of trouble!

Ariel loves to collect human objects she finds on sunken ships and the ocean floor. She stores her collection of treasures in a secret underwater grotto, close to the palace.

A telescope makes a good hat!

Sebastian is Triton's loyal crab composer and is supposed to watch over Ariel. He tries hard but finds it difficult to keep up with her!

Ariel consults her funny seagull friend, Scuttle, about all human things. He claims to be an expert!

Her fins help her to swim fast.

Exploring

Even if it means swimming into dangerous, shark-infested waters, Ariel cannot resist the temptation to explore the ocean for shipwrecks so that she can add to her amazing collection of human things.

Her eyes are as blue as the ocean.

Seashell bikini top

Ariel's hair is the color of red sea anemones and floats in the water.

The tiny scales on her tail shimmer like sequins.

King Triton cannot understand his youngest daughter's love for humans. He thinks that they are dangerous and forbids her to go exploring.

I don't see how a world that makes such wonderful things could be bad!

About Ariel

- She's adventurous and curious.
- Headstrong and impulsive, Ariel refuses to listen to her father.
- She is romantic and gives up her voice for love.
- Ariel is funny and brave.

★ Under the sea ★

Deep under the ocean is a marvelous world of brightly-coloured fish, corals and seaweeds, and a sparkling palace that is home to King Triton and his mermaid daughters. But danger lurks underwater too, if only Ariel would listen.

Ariel shares her bedroom with her six older sisters named Aquata, Andrina, Arista, Attina, Adella, and Alana. Sometimes Ariel finds it hard to be the youngest because everyone treats her like a child!

The underwater palace

Ariel and her sisters' bedroom

King Triton loves Ariel dearly and is prepared to give up everything he has to save her from Ursula, the sea witch.

King Triton's magnificent throne room

Treasures of the deep

Ariel is fascinated by all things from the human world, but she knows her father will be angry if he finds out about her secret collection. She loves to examine the many objects in her cave and imagines what each thing is for.

Ursula

Ursula hates King Triton. The octopus-like sea witch longs to overthrow him so that she can become Queen of the Sea.

Ursula's spies, Flotsam and Jetsam, discover that Ariel is in love with Prince Eric and tell the sea witch. Ursula uses this to her advantage and offers Ariel a cruel deal.

Arches and tunnels are made from sea coral.

Giant clam shells make wonderful instruments in the concert hall.

On dry land

URSULA USES HER MAGIC TO MAKE ARIEL HUMAN and in exchange, Ariel gives up her beautiful voice. To stay human, Ariel must make Eric give her a kiss of true love within three days. If she fails, she will belong to Ursula. But Ariel doesn't realize that Ursula is up to no good and plans to use Ariel's voice to make Eric marry her! Luckily for Ariel, her friends and her father save the day.

Prince Eric

Ariel sees Prince Eric for the first time as his magnificent ship sails past. It is the prince's birthday and the crew celebrates with fireworks.

A violent storm throws the prince overboard but Ariel rescues him and takes him to the shore. She falls deeply in love with Eric but cannot survive on land for long and quickly returns to the sea.

As soon as Ariel drinks Ursula's magic potion, her tail disappears and in its place are two legs. It takes Scuttle a while to work out what's different about her!

Ariel loves being able to walk through the town square, and enjoys talking to all the people.

In the castle kitchen, the chef is determined to catch Sebastian and serve him up for dinner!

Without a voice, it is difficult for Ariel to get the prince to fall in love with her and kiss her.

Roof-garden

Ariel's bedroom

The town

The sea view from the dining room means Ariel is never far from home.

Eric's ship

When King Triton sees how much Ariel and Prince Eric love each other, he allows them to get married.

Belle

BELLE, WHOSE NAME MEANS BEAUTY IN FRENCH, knows that true beauty lies within. But even her goodness is tested when she first sets eyes on the hideous-looking beast who lives in the enchanted castle. Although she doesn't know it, Belle's loving nature and intelligence have the power to transform the Beast into a handsome prince who will make her his princess bride.

ABOUT BELLE
♥ She is loyal and gives up her freedom for the father she adores.
♥ She's clever and makes her own judgments.
♥ She is imaginative and loves to read stories.

I've just finished a wonderful story!

✳ Village friends

Belle's only true friends in the village are the heroes and heroines she meets in the books she loves to read.

Although some people in the village think that Maurice is just a crazy old man, Belle has total faith in her father.

Dancing in this stunning gown, she is truly Belle of the ball.

Her long silky hair is the color of chocolate.

Her big brown eyes are full of warmth.

The rose is a symbol of Belle's love for the Beast.

✳ Castle friends

Lumiere and Cogsworth are two of the castle servants who are changed into household objects by an enchantress. They hope Belle will help them turn back into humans again.

Mrs. Potts, the kindly cook, and Chip, her playful son, cheer Belle up when she first arrives. They think that Belle is just the kind of girl to look beyond first appearances.

✳ Special clothes

At the castle, the Wardrobe provides Belle with all the clothes she could possibly want.

Belle loves the beautiful fur-lined cloak that the Wardrobe gives her. She wears the cloak when she goes walking with the Beast in the beautiful snowy gardens. They have lots of fun playing in the snow and Belle realizes how nice the Beast really is.

Belle's world

BELLE LIVES WITH HER father in a quiet little town where nothing ever happens, and she longs for adventure and a little romance. She soon discovers that not far away lies an enchanted castle and a very different world.

The head of the lunatic asylum calls to take Maurice away.

Belle's house is on the outskirts of town, making her an outsider in more ways than one.

✳ Gaston's admirers

No matter how hard they try, the three village girls cannot get Gaston to notice them. He only has eyes for the beautiful Belle.

The other girls in the village are not as pretty as Belle.

With her nose in a book all day long, Belle hardly notices the things that go on in the town around her. She dreams of a different life far, far away.

Maurice sets off for the fair and rides unsuspectingly into the spooky forest.

Which way? Maurice gets losts when he takes the wrong turn.

The Beast's castle

In the West Wing Belle discovers the enchanted rose.

The bookshop

The village square and fountain

The inn

Gaston and the villagers go on the rampage through the forest to find the Beast and destroy him.

Inside the inn, Gaston and Le Fou plot how to capture Belle's heart.

Learning to love

At FIRST, BELLE IS DESPERATELY UNHAPPY at being imprisoned in the castle, but soon learns to love the enchanted objects. Taming the bad-tempered Beast takes longer and what she doesn't know is that time is running out. The Beast must learn to love and be loved before the last petal of the enchanted rose falls or he will remain a Beast forever.

Gaston and the Beast

Gaston may be handsome to look at, but when he proposes Belle is horrified at the thought of marrying such a vain and stupid man.

Belle is a beauty by nature as well as by name.

Belle loves her father so much that, although scared, she promises to stay in the Beast's castle forever so her father can be free.

Belle finds her evening meal is very entertaining!

The magical servants are overjoyed to welcome Belle to the enchanted castle. She is the first guest they have had for years!

☀ His true nature

When the Beast learns to
control his temper, Belle
sees the kind and loving
person within.

The Beast
grants Belle her
freedom so that
she can help
her father. This is a sign
of his true love for her because he
is willing to give up his only
chance of becoming human again.
This act of kindness makes Belle
realize how much she loves him.

*Belle manages
to uncover
the Beast's
true nature.*

☀ The transformation

The Beast is terribly wounded
by Gaston and Belle fears she
is too late to save him.
Tearfully she confesses her
love for him and the spell
is broken. The Beast regains
his appearance as a handsome
prince and all the enchanted
objects become humans again.

*Belle loves the
Beast no matter
what he looks like.*

Jasmine

BROUGHT UP IN A LIFE OF LUXURY, Jasmine cannot bear being a princess. It's so boring! She longs for adventure and excitement and to be free to make her own choices. The last thing Jasmine wants is to marry a silly, dull prince as the law and her father say she must. When she meets Aladdin, she knows for sure that she could only marry someone she loves.

A sparkling sapphire is fixed upon her headband.

♥ Likes

Jasmine's father is the Sultan of Agrabah and wants only the best for his daughter, including a prince for a husband.

At first Abu is rude to Jasmine but she soon becomes very fond of the cheeky monkey.

Rajah is Jasmine's pet tiger and her closest friend in the palace. She tells him all her secrets and dreams.

Her long, flowing hair is as smooth as satin.

She loves to wear her beautiful pink silk pants.

Her chiffon wrap shimmers in the light.

Her slippers are made of gold.

♥ Dislikes

ABOUT JASMINE

♥ Fiercely independent—she longs to be free and able to make her own choices.

♥ She's brave and isn't afraid to stand up to Jafar and speak her own mind!

♥ She's adventurous and intelligent.

Jafar, the evil vizier and assistant to Jasmine's father, will never win her affection, no matter how powerful he is.

If I do marry I want it to be for love.

Jasmine hates not being free to go where she chooses. She decides to see for herself what life is like on the other side of the palace walls.

Jasmine is not impressed when her father introduces her to Prince Ali because she doesn't recognize Aladdin in his princely clothes. Jasmine is determined to choose her own husband.

Aladdin may be poor, but to Jasmine he is a prince.

Agrabah

JASMINE LIVES IN THE DESERT CITY of Agrabah, in a splendid palace with her father. It is a wonderful city of mystery and enchantment, but she has never been outside the palace walls. Jasmine longs to experience the noise and excitement of the lively city for herself.

Hold on tight for a bird's eye view of Jasmine's world!

The city

In the market place, the merchant isn't pleased when Jasmine gives an apple to a hungry child without realizing she should pay for it!

In the throne room, there is a hidden door that leads up to Jafar's secret lair. He goes there to think up ways to overthrow the Sultan.

The golden minarets glow in the sunlight.

Jafar's secret lair

The Sultan's palace is surrounded by beautiful, exotic gardens. But even in these gardens Jasmine feels trapped and wants to see the city that lies beyond the palace walls.

Aladdin's secret hideaway is on the rooftop of an old, abandoned building. He has amazing views of the whole city and can even see the Sultan's palace.

The Sultan's palace

In the desert, on the outskirts of the city, the Cave of Wonders appears. The cave is filled with precious jewels and treasures. It is here that Aladdin finds the Magic Lamp.

The dungeon is located underneath the palace. This is where Aladdin is held after he is arrested by Jafar's men.

Eastern magic 💚

💚 **I**T MAY NOT LOOK LIKE much on the outside, but when Aladdin rubs the dirty old lamp, an all-powerful Genie appears. The Genie can grant his new master three wishes and could make Aladdin as powerful as the Sultan. But all Aladdin wants is to marry Jasmine—and in the end he doesn't need magic or the Genie to make her love him.

The Genie shows off his strength.

💚 The Genie

The Genie feels a little cramped inside the tiny lamp, his home for the last 10,000 years.

It feels good to be out after all those years inside the lamp!

The Genie understands Jasmine's longing for freedom. Like her, he wants to be able to make his own choices and be his own master. Although the Genie is powerful, he can only grant other people's wishes—not his own.

The Genie has phenomenal cosmic powers.

The Magic Carpet can fly faster than the wind!

Jasmine loves to see the world by air.

 ## The Magic Carpet

Stuck in the Cave of Wonders, Aladdin and Abu might never have escaped if it were not for the Magic Carpet. Although shy and timid at first, the Carpet becomes their friend and helps them escape from danger.

Iago is Jafar's noisy, bad-tempered parrot.

Aladdin's first wish is that he be turned into the wealthy Prince Ali. After Jafar has been defeated, Aladdin has his final wish. He asks that the Genie be set free from the lamp.

Jafar steals the Magic Lamp and the Genie is forced to obey his evil wishes. Aladdin knows that Jafar craves power, and cleverly tricks him into wishing to be a genie. Jafar's wish comes true and he becomes trapped in the lamp forever.

May all your wishes come true!

LONDON, NEW YORK, MELBOURNE,
MUNICH AND DELHI

Designer *Cathy Tincknell*

Project Editor *Lindsay Fernandes*

Written by *Naia Bray-Moffatt*

Art Director *Mark Richards*

Publishing Manager *Cynthia O'Neill Collins*

DTP Designer *Eric Shapland*

Category Publisher *Alex Kirkham*

Production Controller *Nicola Torode*

Additional Art *Marco Colletti, Silvano Scolari and Vincenzo Genna*

This US edition 2006

First American Edition, 2003
03 04 05 06 07 08 10 9 8 7 6 5 4 3 2 1

Published in the United States by
DK Publishing, Inc.
375 Hudson Street
New York, New York 10014

ISBN 13: 978-0-7566-3055-3

Color reproduction by Media Development and Printing, Ltd.
Printed and bound in Mexico by R.R. Donnelley and Sons Co

Discover more at
www.dk.com